CONTENTS

Introduction

Britain became the technological leader of Europe towards the end of the eighteenth century. More and more industrialists from other countries wanted to visit Britain and learn about its technological advances. Among these were the Swedes who had long dominated the European iron market. To produce iron, the iron ore (rock containing iron) was first mined from the ground. It then had to be heated to a high temperature in a blast furnace to separate the waste rock from the pure molten iron which was run into moulds called pigs. The pig iron was then remelted in a small furnace at a foundry to make it into cast iron, or it was sent to forges to be reheated and hammered into bar or wrought iron.

Probably 90 per cent of the total demand for iron by 1800 was for bar iron rather than cast iron. Forging was the usual way to make bar iron from pig iron, but it was expensive and slow. (At its simplest level, forging meant a man hit a lump of hot pig iron with a large hammer until the pig iron changed into bar or wrought iron which was less brittle and stronger than cast iron.) Henry Cort's invention of puddling and rolling in 1783 was important because it not only allowed pig iron to be turned into bar iron in large quantities but it also allowed coke to be used for smelting. Thus puddling was cheaper than forging in labour and fuel. Britain had unlimited supplies of coal for making coke. Overnight, British ironmasters gained a huge advantage over their Swedish rivals.

The worried ironmasters of Sweden sent Eric Thomas Svedenstierna over to England to find out about the new advances and the state of the iron industry generally. We know very little about Svedenstierna. He was born in 1765 and by 1796 was working for the Jernkontor (Iron Bureau – made up of a permanent staff of financial and technical experts). He was sent to France and then to Britain in 1802, returning to Sweden in 1803. He did not write anything of his visit to France but kept a detailed account of his visit to Britain. He thought it was so interesting that as soon as he got back to Sweden he published a book of his journey for the general reader, while he worked on a detailed report for the Jernkontor. He died in 1825.

This book consists of extracts from Svedenstierna's diary of his journey and so gives us a contemporary view of industrial life in England in 1802-3.

Svedenstierna's route around Britain.

SVEDENSTIERNA AND THE
INDUSTRIAL
REVOLUTION

**HISTORY
EYEWITNESS**

EDITED WITH AN INTRODUCTION
AND ADDITIONAL MATERIAL BY
FIONA REYNOLDSON

Published by Heinemann Library,
an imprint of Heinemann Publishers (Oxford) Ltd,
Halley Court, Jordan Hill, Oxford OX2 8EJ

OXFORD LONDON EDINBURGH MADRID
ATHENS BOLOGNA PARIS MELBOURNE
SYDNEY AUCKLAND SINGAPORE TOKYO
IBADAN NAIROBI HARARE GABORONE

This edition is based on a translation of *Svedenstierna's Tour of
Great Britain 1802–3* © David and Charles

Selection and additional material
© Heinemann Publishers (Oxford) Ltd 1993

First published 1993
This edition 1995

99 98 97 96 95
10 9 8 7 6 5 4 3 2 1

British Library Cataloguing in Publication Data is available
from the British Library on request.

ISBN 0 431 07162 4

Designed by Saffron House, map by Jeff Edwards
Printed and bound in China

942.07

Acknowledgements
The publishers would like to thank the following for
permission to reproduce photographs:

Bridgeman Art Library: pp.6, 22, 29
Fotomas Index: p.30
Andrew Fraser, The University of Edinburgh: p.36
Michael Holford: pp.24, 36
Ironbridge Gorge Museum Trust: p.39
Image Select: pp.9, 34, 44
Mansell Collection: p.20, 27, 40
Board of Trustees of the National Museums and Galleries on
Merseyside (Walker Art Gallery): p.43
Nottinghamshire County Library Service: p.19
Tyne & Wear Museums: p.32
Trustees of the Wedgwood Museum: p.15

The cover picture shows Coalbrookdale by night and is reproduced
with the permission of the Bridgeman Art Library.

Every effort has been made to contact copyright holders of material
published in this book. Any omissions will be rectified in subse-
quent printings if notice is given to the publisher.

Note to the reader

In this book some of the words are printed in **bold** type. This indicates that the
word is listed in the glossary on pages 46–7. The glossary gives a brief explanation
of words that may be new to you.

St. Andrews
Fifeshire
Glasgow
Edinburgh
Berwick
R. Tyne
Newcastle
Carlisle
R. Wear
Keswick
York
Hull
Liverpool
Manchester
Sheffield
Derby
Coalbrookdale
Broseley
Birmingham
Bridgenorth
Swansea
Merthyr Tydfil
London
Dover
R. Avon
Bath
R. Kennet
Ilfracombe
Dartmoor
Exeter
St. Austell
Plymouth

North Sea

English Channel

N

0   100 miles
0   200 km

CHAPTER I

To England

Ships off the white cliffs of Dover in 1801. Painted by Thomas Luny.

Towards the end of November 1802 I arrived, via Calais, in Dover. In Calais the traveller must show and sign his passport immediately after arrival, and also have his luggage inspected, the earlier the better. He must at least have his goods taken quickly to the Customs House and from there back on board, whereby something is often lost, or he cannot otherwise depart with the first packet boat. The export of French gold and silver coins is forbidden. It is best, therefore, to change such coins for **guineas** or banknotes, to which end one seeks out the landlord, or even better, a good business house, and entrusts them with the transaction, otherwise in the inns an attempt may be made to cheat the traveller with debased if not counterfeit coins.

As soon as the packet boat arrives at the quay at Dover, the luggage of the passengers is taken to the Customs House, where the owner must declare everything which is dutiable. If this is not done, before inspection, the dutiable goods are confiscated. If, however, one declares everything all the petty annoyances to which a traveller is subjected in some other countries are avoided. Also in Dover the passport must be shown, and one receives a written permit, which

contains a description of the traveller, and is signed by the latter. One must keep this carefully until departure from England, when it will be demanded back by the Aliens Office where the passport is signed upon departure.

Dover is in itself not very remarkable. Here, as in all other places where the packet vessels land, everything is dearer, and travellers who want to go direct to London do best to depart with the first mail coach or other public vehicle. In such case it does not matter at what time of day one approaches the capital. If, however, one travels by one's own coach or by **post-chaise**, it is safer to make sure that one reaches London in daylight, because one is most likely to be robbed near the town itself. Between Dover and London nothing appeared to deserve my special attention except a few small foundries and glass furnaces, besides the shipyard at Chatham and the **powder mills** at Dartford, which however, cannot be seen without special permission.

Upon arrival in London, it is best to stay in the inn where the coach stops, until one has decided upon a lodging. In this, it is necessary to take the advice of someone who knows the town, for one otherwise runs the risk of living in a house of ill fame or in a street which one may not name without exposing oneself to people's scorn. A traveller who has business with the learned institutions and comes into contact with either scholars or with persons of rank, must lodge in the western part of London. He must reckon upon no less a rent than one and a half to two guineas per week. For this rent one gets only the room and its cleaning, and is therefore obliged to employ a servant who, if he is to be kept loyal, also receives one and a half guineas per week. Although it would be possible to eat cheaply in certain tiny taverns and eating houses, it is almost a rule for a foreigner who is seeking good acquaintanceships, to visit the better taverns. One cannot eat at these for less than five shillings per day.

THE WARS WITH FRANCE

There was a revolution in France in 1789 which led to the execution of the king and queen. Other countries in Europe were alarmed by the upheavals in France and war followed. Britain was almost continuously at war with France from 1793. France decided on peace in 1801 and signed a treaty with Austria and Prussia, followed, in 1802, by the Treaty of Amiens with Britain. Peace only lasted about a year during which time travel was much easier for foreigners. This was when Svedenstierna visited France and Britain. In 1803 Napoleon invaded Hanover (in Germany) which had close links with Britain and he also threatened to invade Britain. This was the beginning of the long Napoleonic Wars which lasted until 1815.

As soon as one is settled in, one must procure a plan of London, partly to find one's way about this enormous mass of buildings, partly to find the route to be taken to meet those people with whom one has to talk, in the shortest time and to spend as little as possible on hackney carriages. Besides a plan, a guidebook is necessary. The one which is called *The Picture of London for 1803*, being a correct guide to all the curiosities, amusements etc. is the most reliable. Reading it gives more information about the objects which are notable for a traveller than is given by a person who has lived here for several years.

Travel in whichever land you will, it is always useful to know the whys and wherefores. In England it is essential to have one or two letters of introduction from respected and learned men. I had one from Louis Vauquelin and another from a French mines superintendent. My object was to get to know, as well as I could, the methods of ironmaking in England and the works connected with it. With this in mind, I settled into my life in London, using my letters of introduction to meet leading scholars and to see private collections of minerals. Among the places to which I gained access were the Royal Institution and the Royal Society. The Royal Institution is situated in a large house in Albemarle Street and consists of workshops, reading rooms and lecture theatres. Two professors are employed full time, that is one for chemistry, Professor Davy, and one for mechanics and physics. A talk about the uses and applications of chemistry, with which Professor Davy opened his lectures last winter, surpassed everything I had previously heard of scientific eloquence, not even excepting Fourcroy's lectures. And thus the throng of listeners of both sexes and of all classes became so great that one always had to be there in good time, in order to get a seat.

The Royal Society is too well known to need any description. A foreigner who is acquainted with a member is easily admitted to the weekly meetings. Last winter a series of luncheons were held on meeting days in a tavern near to Somerset House. They were presided over often by the permanent president, Joseph Banks. Once or twice I took part with much pleasure in this learned meal.

Portrait of Sir Humphry (Professor) Davy. Born in Cornwall in 1778 he left school when his father died and was apprenticed to a doctor. However, he became very interested in the study of chemistry and was soon put in charge of a laboratory in Bristol investigating the effects of different gases on people. He discovered the effects of nitrous oxide or 'laughing gas' in preventing pain. At the age of 21, he was made an assistant at the Royal Institution London and soon became famous as a brilliant lecturer. Davy was knighted in 1812 and in 1815 invented the miner's safety lamp for which he is still famous. Although nowadays miners use electric lamps, Davy's lamp is still used for testing the level of methane in the air in mines.

CHAPTER 2

Journey to the South West

A Royal Mail coach. This print was first published in 1805.

After I had spent the winter months in visiting such places as the Royal Society and the British Museum and had made not only a good circle of acquaintances, but also obtained some practice in the language of the country, I decided in February to undertake the journey to the ironworks.

However, I soon found that it was extremely difficult to obtain the information necessary for this purpose. Neither those who dealt in iron nor those who owned ironworks could tell me exactly which route I would have to take in order to see the most and the largest ironworks, or what difficulties a foreigner might encounter and so on. Despairingly I sought information about ironworks in the guides and travel-books, of which a great number are available. These contain more or less wearisome descriptions of churches, castles, views etc which indeed could be edifying for other tourists, but were of no use at all to me. I had therefore almost decided to go straight to Scotland, where I was provided by a friend with introductions to some ironworks. Meantime I came to speak to Mr Charles Greville of my difficulties and he not only offered me introductions to the largest ironworks of the kingdom, but also gave me an extract from his mineralogical notes which he had collected on a tour of south Wales and Cornwall. It is true that my actual destination was not Cornwall where there were no ironworks, but because Mr Greville represented to me that a journey there would be interesting and, at the same time suggested as a travelling companion a French *Ingénieur des Mines*, M. Bonnard, whose

acquaintance I had already made, I thought that this detour was acceptable in order afterwards to be able to see the things which were the principal object of my tour. Mr Charles Greville's patronage was excellent and I would be in good company.

Before setting out I collected as much information as I could, including guide books and a good map of England, for at a distance of a few miles from the most noteworthy place, one can probably ask a hundred persons the way to it, without finding anyone who knows anything about it. Besides it is necessary to show the names in writing for the English often do not know how a name is pronounced in different places.

With our letters of introduction from Mr Greville and from, among other of his friends, the Duke of Devonshire, we left London on 1 March 1803. We decided to go direct to Exeter which is about 27 Swedish miles from the capital. I must remark, for the information of other tourists, that when one books a seat in a coach from London, it is necessary to inquire minutely at the coach office, about the quality of the coach and by which route it goes. If one travels with the Royal Mail, which belongs to the Post Office, this is not necessary; we, however, for the sake of economy, booked places on another coach. When we arrived in Piccadilly, where we were supposed to board, we found the coach packed so full of passengers that I was obliged to speak to the coachman in a serious tone before two gentlemen were forced to make room for us by sitting on the roof.

THE ROYAL MAIL

The increasing business generated by the growth in Britain's industry led to demands for a better postal service. In 1784 Thomas Palmer, tired of the slow stage-coach service between London and Bath, where he had a business, proposed a new type of coach. These coaches carried only four inside passengers so the load for the four horses was less. The quality of the horses was better and the teams were changed every seven or eight miles, sometimes only taking thirty seconds to change. As a result the times taken over long journeys were almost halved. The cost of running the coaches was higher, but more and more business people appreciated the faster speeds (and the armed guard) and were prepared to pay a higher fare. The Post Office gave the contract for carrying mail to the new coaches and by 1800 there were regular services all over the country with the Royal Mail keeping to a strict timetable. Letters posted one day on the main routes could be delivered 120 miles away the next morning.

Furthermore we discovered that the coach went via Bath where we did not want to go at all. However, that apart, one travels better in these country coaches than in any kind of Swedish hired vehicle, and the only problem is the necessity to take good care of one's luggage, for these coaches carry a great number of packages and suitcases. Although we did not here travel in such good company as on the better post coaches, we came in good time to Bath, where we caught the Flying Coach (a light and very fast vehicle) which brought us punctually to Exeter.

We found on the way nothing more remarkable (from our point of view) than a few small canals near Bath, which flow into the Kennet and Avon Canal connecting the two rivers of the same names and opening up communication right across England, between the Severn and the Thames estuaries.

Potters at work. This print was first published in 1805.

A few miles from Exeter around the town of Neuton Bushel [now Newton Abbot] the district is low and enclosed by hills. At one of these hills, lime is burnt in specially erected furnaces of two types of construction. The one kind was similar to our blast-furnace shafts, it was eighteen feet deep and rather wide in proportion. The other kind of **limekiln**, which is more frequently met with in England, was only fourteen to fifteen feet deep and had the form of an inverted cone. The burning is usually done with the coal and chalk put in in layers, as in a blast furnace. When the lime is ready, it is hooked out at the bottom, and a fresh charge put in at the top. Sometimes, when the lime is to be used for **mortar**, the requisite quantity of sand is mixed with it.

Not far from here there are some clay-pits, partly for an earthenware factory nearby at Bovey Tracey, partly for earthenware factories at

places as far way as Stafford and Worcester. This clay is of two kinds, either black or grey-brown, but both become white on **firing**. Above this good clay lies another mixed with sand which is good enough for making bricks.

In order to get to Dartmoor we took our way to Moreton Hampstead where we came upon an open mine of a substance that looked like pulverised **plumbago** or **graphite** but which has been found on accurate chemical analysis to be a kind of iron ore. It is called here the 'shining ore' and is sold at six guineas a ton, being particularly useful for the cleaning and polishing of certain cast iron objects, such as steam cylinders, hotplates etc., which not only thereby receive a fine appearance but are also protected from rust.

On our way to Plymouth we passed many tin mines which are now little worked. We took up our night quarters near the docks at Plymouth, from where we wanted to go the next morning by water to

Torpoint and from there direct to St Austell in Cornwall. We should both have liked to see over the shipyards but it is not generally permitted to a foreigner and in the present-day state of affairs, it would have been imprudent to ask. However, the next morning we passed between the warships lying in the harbour and had a beautiful view of Plymouth Sound, the town and harbour.

St Austell itself is a small town, with narrow, winding streets, but it is lively on account of the nearby tin mines and **smelting** works. We were here recommended to a Mr Charles Rashleigh who not only possesses many important mines but is also known for his patriotic works. He has for instance, built a fine harbour here with a high wall against the sea and several docks, a large inn for the benefit of seafarers and a long alley with little houses for the workpeople, to say nothing of the warehouse, brickworks and limekilns.

We continued on our way to the clay-pits of St Stephens, from which the white fireproof clay used for the genuine **porcelain** wares which were recently introduced is dug out. It is also used in the great Wedgwood Etruria factory in Staffordshire. Nearby, the white, **translucent**, and grainy substance called **feldspar** is quarried. It is mixed with the porcelain mass in order to bring about an incomplete fusion during the firing, whereby, the porcelain receives a **glazed** surface and becomes translucent at the edges. These two substances seem to me very similar to those which I had seen in the manufactories of Sèvres and Paris. The discovery of this clay is very important for it has led to the founding of the famous works at Etruria and to the increase in factory-made pottery which daily bring such enormous sums into England.

The clay is found just below the surface and is dug out with spades, at a depth of eight to nine feet (at least they have not yet needed to go any deeper). The spadefuls are taken to washing troughs and drying houses. Here one or more lumps are thrown into a trench with running water, and there crushed with the spade. Whereupon, during the continuous stirring the pure clay is separated and washed away with the water to the settling house. The clay then goes through several settling ponds, set one above the other, until it comes into the lower pit of the drying house. When all the water has run away, the clay is allowed to lie for a few more days, after which it is lifted out in large cubic pieces, and when thoroughly dry, packed into casks. It is then ready to be used for porcelain mixes.

The feldspar which is used in porcelain manufacture is no less remarkable. It occurs in the same valley but I could not find out exactly how it is prepared before it is added to the porcelain mix, although I do not believe there is anything secret about it. Like the

Part of a Wedgwood tea service in Pearl Ware (a variety of earthenware) made between about 1805 and 1810.

clay, the feldspar is packed in casks and then taken overland to Charlestown, from there shipped to Liverpool, and finally despatched over the inland canals to several factories in Staffordshire, Worcester, Shropshire etc.

M. Bonnard and I decided to cross by water to south Wales and made our way up through Cornwall to a little harbour on the Bristol Channel, named Ilfracombe, from whence a packet boat departs twice or three times a week for Swansea. In case our unusual route should excite mistrust or we ran into difficulties, we were provided with letters of introduction from a Member of Parliament for Barnstaple to Mr Gribble and from Mr Gribble to one of his friends in Ilfracombe.

The packet boat was unfortunately over at Swansea and had not been able to return for several days on account of storms. We waited for a couple of days and then hired for five guineas a little vessel of the kind usually used for smuggling, and here called skiffs. When one agrees upon such a sea voyage, one must lay down the conditions in advance. Because we had omitted to come to a clear agreement with the skipper, we got an Irish officer for company who should have paid his share of the fee and did not.

The crossing took only three hours, but on arrival at Swansea the tide had already gone out so far that we could only come within a mile and a half of the harbour. We were therefore landed at a place called Oystermouth, from whence we had our goods transported to the town on a cart hauled by four oxen, for seven English shillings.

South Wales

COKE

Much of the coal mined near Swansea was turned into coke. The coal is heated in ovens with as little air as possible so it does not burn. This changes the coal into coke which is almost pure carbon. Coke rather than coal is burnt in the furnaces used to get pig iron from iron ore (rock), because the smoky impurities in coal would harm the iron-making process. Producing coke and using it to smelt iron ore was pioneered by Abraham Darby.

SMELTING IRON ORE

Iron is separated from the ore by smelting in a blast furnace. The furnace is fed with a mixture of the ore (rock), limestone and coke. The coke burns firecely and the heat removes the oxygen from the iron ore. As the oxygen is removed the iron melts and trickles down to the bottom of the furnace. The sand, clay and other impurities in the ore react with the limestone to form a liquid slag which floats on top of the liquid iron in the furnace. This liquid iron is called pig iron.

The harbour of Swansea is noteworthy on account of its spaciousness and the works which have been built and which are still in hand for the protection of ships. All the building is being done at the expense of the town of Swansea, which a few decades ago was of little importance, but in recent years, through the rich coalmines, mines and factories in the neighbourhood, has risen to a great prosperity.

By far the greatest riches are the coal seams, about whose depth and situation not everyone yet seems to be agreed. Yet there is no doubt about the fact that they are encountered in an almost unbroken chain over a length of more than 100 miles and 3 to 4 miles in breadth. Besides coal, **ironstone**, sandstone, clay and limestone for 42 blast furnaces (of which each produces 2,000 tons of pig iron annually) these coal seams provide enough coal for the production of 6,000 to 7,000 tons of copper which is produced at 14 copper works around Swansea and the Neath canal.

Men loading coal. This print was first published in 1805.

It is remarkable that these coal deposits were little worked up till 30 or 40 years ago and that on this bare heathland which still 20 years ago merely grazed goats, there now live thousands of people, whose work brings millions of pounds into the country, and contributes to a high degree to its culture and growth.

To return to Swansea, one finds near the town such a profusion of copper works, coalmines, steam engines, ponds, canals, **aqueducts** and railways, that the traveller becomes quite undecided where to start or how to make order of the chaos. For one seeks in vain for information from passers-by, who seldom know their nearest neighbours by name. We were recommended to a retired copper refiner who lived on his estate near a town which he had founded, called Morristown. We were thus able to visit many mines and enquire about methods of working. On these excursions we saw the following, which may deserve the attention of a tourist.

SOUTH WALES

Eighteenth century Wales was almost entirely rural until the development of the coal and iron resources in south Wales dramatically changed the way in which people lived and the numbers of people living there. However, there were very few people in Wales itself who could afford to invest in the expensive new steam engines and other machines needed to extract the coal and iron, so the men who opened up the mines and smelting works were often merchants from England. Anthony Bacon, a London merchant, set up the Cyfarthfa iron works at Merthyr Tydfil in 1765. Although Welsh businessmen moved in too, they are often found in partnership with English merchants who had made their money in foreign trade.

The Shipping on the River Tawe

This river is not considered important but for the fact that first of all it partially provides the copper works, and in particular the steam engines, with the necessary water, and secondly, it is navigable for fairly large ships for some distance up from the estuary. These go up and down with the tide, and, at several landing places built along the river, either take on coal or unload copper ore and other goods, which are then transported farther inland on the canals or railways.

The railways or 'roads of iron'

The transport of coal from the nearest mines down to the ships is done over a railway specially laid for the purpose, which is laid at such a gradient that two waggons carrying about thirteen hundredweights of coal each run forwards by their own weight. They are restrained in their journey by a brake fitted to the rear waggon, applied by a man who travels with the waggons to deal with the unloading. The waggon comes down the hill and runs forward on a bridge built into the river; this has a large opening or hole in it so that the part of the ship to be loaded can lie centrally beneath it. The laden waggon rolls over this opening, and its bottom is opened by pulling out a pin, whereupon the coal falls down into the ship. The empty waggons are afterwards coupled together in a train, and hauled up over the same way by a horse. This railway is about one and a half miles from the river. From the more distant mines the coal is first taken over such inclined railways or by the network of small canals. Occasionally the boats go a mile or so underground, and take on their load of coal in the mine itself.

Railways, which one now encounters in the whole of England run all over the place between the canals and the works. They either run downhill or are pulled by horses. Although these ways are all alike at a first glance, they are actually of two kinds. The one kind are called railroads or railways and consist of iron bars two to three inches wide. They are smooth on the upper and inner edges but can have any form on the under and outer sides. The waggons have **flanges** on the inside edges of the wheels so the rolling waggon is held on the rails. The other kind are called tramroads or tramways. The track is made of iron bars which have a turned up flange on the outer side. This prevents the ordinary wheel, like a wheelbarrow wheel, from falling off the rails.

The canals and aqueducts

Beside the five-feet deep and ten-feet-wide Swansea Canal, which stretches for some miles up country beside the River Tawe, there are several small canals and aqueducts, which partly carry water to the surrounding works, and partly carry the small boats. There is a network of these little canals, the smaller ones crossing the large by means of aqueducts. In other places the aqueducts pass under the large canals by means of stone-built **culverts**, either to carry the water away from the mines, or to provide the steam engines and the copper mines with water.

The steam engines

It is not too much to say these engines are as common in England as are watermills and windmills with us, and are found in far greater numbers. Also they come in all possible sizes and of both better and

Canal and road in the early nineteenth century. Notice the turnpike gate across the road where both the coach and the cart will have to pay a toll (small sum of money) to use the road. There were tolls on canals as well.

Men working at puddling. Stirring the hot iron was part of the process. A nineteenth century engraving.

worse construction. Around Swansea they are used for many different purposes. Some pump water out of the coalmines, others haul coal to the surface, and still others set in motion rolling mills, stamping machines etc. Several were old and of a less pleasing appearance, and consumed much coal, to which they paid little attention at the mines, nor did they need to do so.

However, the engine at Clandower [Landore? – Svedenstierna has obviously misunderstood the pronounciation of this word] deserves special mention. It was built according to Boulton and Watt's latest **patent**, with the strength of 70 or 80 horses and lifted the water out of a coal mine from a depth of 48 fathoms. The normal speed was about 12 strokes per minute; it could, however, in an emergency be taken up to 60. It was calculated that it moved overall 1,100 gallons in a minute.

The hard porcelain factory

This, which belongs to a Mr George Haynes, deserves to be seen. In this works are made teacups, basins, plates etc. painted in complete imitation of the coarse blue Chinese porcelain. Although other things such as beermugs are made here and some finer goods, the blue porcelain is sold at such good prices in America and other places abroad that in a year, Mr Haynes cannot make as much as is ordered.

On 18 or 19 March we left Swansea and took our way to Merthyr Tydfil. We visited an unremarkable ironworks producing low grade pig iron and saw several other ironworks from the post chaise as we travelled through the hilly countryside. At one coal mine we passed we saw an interesting railway. The waggons sent down the railway were controlled by a very simple machine. This machine consisted of a horizontal roller, around which a double rope was wound. When the loaded waggon came down from the mine, it was hooked fast on one end of the rope. Then not only did it run down the slope to the canal itself, but also pulled the empty waggon, which was fastened to the other end of the rope, up the hill to the mine again. In order to moderate the speed, the end of the roller was braked by an iron brake shoe, which could comfortably be done by one man.

Merthyr Tydfil, which a few decades ago was an unimportant place has, through its great ironworks, become one of the most remarkable places in England. In an area about three miles long and one wide are thirteen blast furnaces which produce weekly something like 40 tons of pig iron and **castings**. Besides that there are 20,000 tons of **wrought iron**, hoop iron, bolt iron and sheets prepared here annually.

Notwithstanding all this, the production could only with difficulty have been pushed so high if they had not here adopted the so-called puddling process, which was invented some 20 years ago by an Englishman named Cort, afterwards tried out in several places in England, and had almost been abandoned again, when it was finally brought to perfection through the persistent efforts of Mr Crawshay of Cyfarthfa. This unique process has now been adopted for some years with various modifications in England, Scotland and Ireland.

The number of workshops in all the ironworks is unknown to me, but at Pen-y-daren alone there are three **blast furnaces**, three **refineries**, twenty-five puddling and eight bloom furnaces, plus the necessary hammers and rolling mills, as well as nine or ten steam engines. It is said that the number of workers here is about nine hundred and in all four ironworks there are about four thousand workers including the miners. One can imagine how small this number is by comparison with that which would be necessary in Sweden for such great production.

Mr Homfray has laid down a railway of about ten miles that runs close to the Cardiff Canal. When I expressed my astonishment that they had laid down a railway in the same direction as the canal, I was assured that the cost was fully recouped by the saving in **lock dues** and in time. The lock dues are six pence per ton for every mile. With the cost of maintaining the boats and other expenses it amounts to about twelve shillings and six pence to transport a ton of goods for the whole twenty-three miles of the canal to Cardiff.

HENRY CORT'S PUDDLING PROCESS

Henry Cort devised the puddling process whereby molten pig iron was stirred with rods. This helped remove impurities. The pasty mass was then hammered with a water-powered hammer. The result was large quantities of good quality bar iron. Together with Cort's invention of rolling mills for rolling the iron, this led to a huge increase in iron production.

CHAPTER 4

The Midlands

The ironworks at Coalbrookdale by night. Painted by P.J. de Loutherbourg in 1801.

Broseley is a little town in Shropshire lying on the southern bank of the River Severn. It is surrounded by coalmines and ironstone **quarries**, some of which are even worked in and under the town itself. On the slopes, close to the river, lie several ironworks and foundries, lime and brick **kilns** and other plants and factories which form an unbroken chain of buildings from Broseley up to the famous iron bridge near Coalbrookdale (see the following pages). The Dale Works have their beginning close by the entrance to Coalbrookdale and stretch up the valley. Here are made a quantity of fine castings, such as

STEAM ENGINES

Svedenstierna obviously encountered on his travels round the mines both the older Newcomen steam engines, which used a great deal of coal and the improved Watt engines.

Thomas Newcomen had improved the design of existing steam engines in 1705 and his engines were widely used to pump water out of the mines between 1720 and 1800. Steam from a boiler pushed a piston up. When cold water was squirted on the steam it cooled, condensed and the water took up less room than the steam so the piston dropped down. This action was repeated constantly.

In 1763, James Watt was mending a Newcomen engine and noticed the waste of heat caused by constantly re-heating the steam. He decided that the answer was to keep the part where steam had to remain steam hot, and the part where steam was condensed, cold. This cut down the large coal consumption and was welcomed in places like the Cornish tin mines, far from coal fields. About 40 of Watt's engines were in use for pumping water out of these mines by 1800. They were to affect the iron industry also, as they raised water to turn wheels to operate machinery at the iron foundries and forges.

firegrates, weights, **flatirons**, **stoves**, screws for cider presses and the like. Some of the articles are cast from small **cupola furnaces**, wherein small **ingots** and all kinds of broken scrap are melted down with normal blast. Furnaces like this can be seen in London and in nearly every foundry in the country. Often they are driven by a small cylinder blower, which is worked by horses. All the main blast furnaces and rolling mills at the Dale Works are driven by the usual large steam engines, but the **lathes** and grinding machines are operated by the water of a brook, which winds through the valley.

I was interested to see at a coalmine near here a small steam engine of only three **horsepower**. Its job was to haul coal up from a few fathoms below ground. The boiler for this little engine was put in the chimney **ventilator** of the mine so that a special fire for ventilating the mine was saved.

Among the things which here commonly first attract the attention of the traveller, is the iron bridge. I am afraid that I no longer remember the length of the arch, which is anyway described in many places. However, I must mention one incident which bears witness to the strength of such bridges. Some time earlier, the ground at one end had yielded, yet people drove over the bridge without noticing, until some bolts had either broken or bent and it could be seen that parts of the bridge were separating. These parts were screwed together, the arch tightened up, the displaced **abutment** strengthened and all this without the bridge once becoming unusable. The iron bridge is less remarkable now, since finer and larger ones have been built in England; however, it was the first of its kind and convinced most people to such an extent that Parliament has agreed to an iron bridge over the Thames, in place of London Bridge.

The iron bridge at Coalbrookdale over the river Severn was the first bridge in the world made of iron. Built in 1779 it consisted of five parallel arch ribs almost 200 feet in length.

The mines here are not deep, not more than ten fathoms, often less. The method of working is quite simple: first of all the coal is taken out and afterwards as much ironstone as is required, after which the mine is abandoned. Everywhere in this district collapsed shafts and depressions in the earth can be encountered, even where there are houses and gardens. Some houses were in fact broken down, or so slantwise, that I could not conceive how anyone could live in them.

A bare three miles from Ironbridge lies the ironworks of Lightmoor, the head of which is a Mr Homfray, brother of the Mr Homfray at Pen-y-daren. It consists of three blast furnaces, some refineries and bloom or ball furnaces. Here the principal purpose is to make good iron and the manager of the works asserted that it sold for up to £26 a ton to people like Mr Boulton junior of Soho [Birmingham] for use in making steam engines. He told me that they often used the Lightmoor iron instead of the best Swedish, not because it was in general better, but because the quality was more reliable.

After looking at some railways and at the barges on the Shropshire Canal we left Coalbrookdale and continued our journey to Birmingham, through Shifnal, Wolverhampton and Wednesbury. We passed three large ironworks and I would very much like to have seen Ketteley which belongs to Mr Raynolds. However, if in England one has no special letter of introduction and, as a stranger, presents oneself in the company of a Frenchman, one can expect nothing but a polite refusal. I found this answer so correct that I could not press any further to see the works. From Wolverhampton, where we arrived in good time in the afternoon, we immediately made an excursion to the nearby ironworks. These are generally on a smaller scale than those of south Wales or Coalbrookdale. The type of production is more divided too. Some **ironmasters** have furnaces, others have foundries and still other have puddling and rolling mills, rather than all being in one big works.

As, late in the evening, we returned to the town of Wolverhampton, we saw the glow of fires from a great number of works in the remarkable plain between Wolverhampton, Wednesbury, Birmingham and Dudley.

The following day the journey went on to Birmingham, which is so famed on account of its factories and on account of the vast quantity of ornamental and metal wares which for 30 years have been distributed from there all over the world. The town has a fine situation in the centre of a rich and cultivated district. Its regular parks, fine buildings, many and large factories, together with the splendid fields and canals which both surround and run through the town, make it one of the most interesting towns in the world.

THE GROWTH OF THE IRON INDUSTRY

In the first half of the eighteenth century the furnaces and foundries had been charcoal fed and had therefore been situated near woodlands and forests. As the production of coke developed, so the coke-fed blast furnaces had been growing in size and number, encouraged by the demand for weapons during the war of 1756–63. Once puddling and rolling developed, using coke to smelt pig iron into bar iron, the forge-masters no longer needed charcoal, and tended to move closer to the furnaces and foundries. In quite a short time, big ironworks were created where the whole process from mining coal and ore to making tools and weapons took place together. Large new communities were created, and the output of iron increased enormously.

Through these canals communication has been opened in recent times between Birmingham and the four great trading towns and seaports of England-London, Liverpool, Hull and Bristol. Certain manufacturing concerns, whose products merely depend upon the mood of fashion, have certainly declined and other towns have in recent years shared profits with Birmingham. But all this cannot be seen by the tourist, who only sees the plain evidence of riches and industry.

My travelling companion had letters from M. Prony in Paris to the famous Watt, who, in partnership with Mr Boulton, has not only brought the steam engine to its present perfection, but has also worked out a large number of mechanical inventions at the great Soho works near Birmingham. This factory which Boulton and Watt have now given over to their sons, is closed to all strangers without exception. We knew this already and merely presented our letters with the intention of obtaining from Mr Watt some general information about the town. Our desire was fulfilled in that his son James Watt suggested an excursion to Dudley upon which he would accompany us.

We therefore met Mr J. Watt the following morning on his estate, a distance from Soho, and thus took the road direct to Dudley Castle, from the heights of which we could look down on the plain between Wolverhampton and Birmingham. One sees here several towns, and a great number of ironworks and factories, coalmines, limekilns etc. and at the same time looking out over the most splendid fields that one can imagine, which are everywhere traversed by canals and highways and settled with pleasant houses and magnificent estates.

One sees perhaps 40 large and small ironworks of which some merely produce pig iron, others only bar iron, nail rods and the like. It is impossible to judge the total output of the works here and just as impossible to get any reliable information about it. However, I believe that I am not far out if I estimate the annual production of these works in wrought iron at around 12,000 tons. Of pig iron I cannot estimate, but to judge from the pig iron which one sees being transported on the canals to Birmingham and other places where there are foundries it must be considerable. All these works obtain their coal and ironstone from the **seams** lying in the plain mentioned above. I could not decide to what extent these seams were connected with those in Shropshire but according to what the people here say, they are separated from the latter by the chalk hills. The thinnest coal seams are from 9 to 14 feet thick and some deeper ones 30 to 40 feet thick but these, which are already being worked lie at a depth of around 50 fathoms. This deep coal is, however not so good as that from the thinner seams. Not only does all this coal and ironstone supply the works around here, but it also supplies many limekilns and is shipped to places like Birmingham

where much is used by the population of some 60,000. The Birmingham Canal earns some £1,000 per week, charging at two shillings a ton on the coal and other goods transported.

We continued on our way to view the Bradley ironworks near Wednesbury which is the property of Mr John Wilkinson. This is the largest in the whole district, consisting of two or three blast furnaces, various re-melting, puddling, and ball-furnaces, rolling mills for bar iron and sheets and shearing mills as well as other installations and workshops. It is asserted that in certain weeks nearly 200 tons of sheets, hoop iron, bars and nail rods were made here. The last-named were sold to the people of the town, who work them by hand, particularly when there is no other work. Wilkinson had some new ways of rolling iron but the bars were rough at the edges, uneven and badly worked and had to go through further processes before they were usable for sheets and ordinary bar iron. Therefore, it is not surprising that few have taken up the inventor's new process.

Boulton and Watts' Factory.
Watt joined Boulton as a partner in the firm in 1775 and the partnership worked well as Boulton was a good business man and Watt could develop his inventions.

On the canal close to the works lay several barges of 20 tons, built
from iron plates, the work of Mr Wilkinson. In general they lay higher
in the water and glided more easily than the wooden ones, remained
fairly watertight and withstood powerful blows, but cost three to four
times as much as a wooden barge. Since a wooden one, with some
maintenance, can be used for 20 years, it is still undecided how this
experiment will pay. Wilkinson is said also to have built a larger vessel
of ironplates on the River Severn, which – I do not know why – turned
out less happily. He was at the time in London so I was unable to make
his acquaintance. He is now an old man, but full of new ideas with
which he is said to have enriched science more than himself.

The canals hereabout are all to the same plan with locks 7 to 8 feet
wide, 50 to 60 feet long and 3,4 or 5 feet deep, partly walled with
brick or dressed stone. The canals are either open ditches with sloping
sides, or walled vertically with bricks, like the Dutch ones. Those
which run through the
town are sometimes
culverted with bricks
over a distance of
several hundred yards
with streets and
houses above them.
One of the canals,
some distance from
the town, crosses over
a fairly large brook by
means of an aqueduct.
They are all provided
with the important
wide and comfortable
towpaths, on one or
both sides. It is easy
to imagine what an
enormous quantity of
bricks is required for
these canals as well as
the buildings in the
towns and around, but
the manufacture keeps
pace with demand
without difficulty.

A kind of clay is found near the town which is already in the right mix. It is just dug out and water run on to it until it is so soft that it can be easily worked. It is stirred up with a spade, and is then ready for moulding. Only invalids, women and children did the work, and a sixteen year old girl asserted that she could mould 3,000 bricks a day. Another girl brought her the clay and a small boy carried the bricks away.

There is no country where a traveller can enjoy every comfort of life with less obstruction; but there are also few lands where a more careful eye is kept upon those who show interest in factories and mechanical installations. At the same time I noticed with satisfaction that as a Swede one could always expect a more open behaviour than could several foreigners, who in recent times, through the secret export of models, and by tempting away the workmen etc. have aroused the most reasonable suspicions against themselves.

A coalmine in the early nineteenth century. Notice that pillars of coal have been left to hold up the roof. Later this was forbidden because it was safer to use pit props. The horse is pulling the coal to the shaft so that it can be hauled to the surface by either steam or horse power.

CHAPTER 5

The North East

Workers preparing crucibles for cast-steel.

It was natural, left to myself, to direct my attention chiefly to those ironworks which I had not yet had an opportunity of seeing. I knew already, before my departure from London that some important ironworks lay in the neighbourhood of Sheffield and in several places in the southern part of Yorkshire, but I had not been able to get any reliable information other than to obtain introductions to the proprietors. It was therefore my intention to go to Hull, in order to get the necessary letters from **Consul** Brandström there and in the meantime to see as much as I could. I took a seat in the Mail Coach direct to Sheffield, which constitutes a day's journey or about 80 miles.

It was already dark before I got to Sheffield, but I was fortunate, upon dismounting from the coach, in making the acquaintance of a **Quaker**, who was a **shareholder** and manager of an ironworks in the town. He sought me out on the following morning and accompanied me to several ironworks.

Sheffield is one of the smaller towns of England, but famous on account of its cast-steel factories and of the quantity of silverware and cutting tools made there. Through the middle of the town runs the River Don, the fall of which is utilized by the rolling, cutting and

polishing works erected here. The river is not navigable and there are no canals nearby so the goods must be transported overland. The value of the goods is such that the cost of a small amount of land transport is of little importance.

The quality of the Sheffield goods is excellent when one considers how difficult it is, in the large scale manufacture of such things, to obtain a large quantity of the same quality. Razors by the hundred dozen are turned out at two and a half English shillings each and sold at ironmongers in London and elsewhere, when inferior ones, not made in Sheffield, cost as much as half a guinea.

However, other kinds of cutting tools are made here too. These goods are but cast in moulds, ground and polished and often have a sharp edge, but break at the tiniest pressure. Some of these are sold 50 per cent cheaper than the equivalent work in steel and in recent times a quantity of them has been exported to both Indies and to several places in Europe. However, the true English patriot is not happy about this trade because it diminishes the profits of those who make the good products and because confidence in the justly famous English cutting wares may be weakened.

As well as visiting the ironworks, I did have the opportunity in Sheffield of observing the cast-steel process fairly closely in two factories. The oldest and largest cast-steel works, which has long been famous, is that of Mr Huntsman in Sheffield and the products of other works have only been comparable for a few years. This is still a little understood field in most countries such as France, Germany and Russia. In England, on the other hand, the practical knowledge of cast-steel is much more general. One encounters little cutlery there which is not made from it, and on my whole tour as well as in my stay in London, I was not able to see a single saw, from the large carpenters' saws several feet long to the smallest surgical ones, which were not made of a type of cast-steel.

THE CAST-STEEL PROCESS

Benjamin Huntsman was a clock maker. He worked out a way to make high quality steel which he needed for making watch springs. Up until then only blister steel was known. Blister steel was made when bar iron and charcoal were heated together in clay pots. This took about three weeks and produced poor quality 'blistered' steel. Huntsman put pieces of the blister steel in crucibles (closed fireclay pots) and burned away all the impurities at a very high temperature in a coke-fired furnace. The resulting steel was called cast-steel and was of a very high quality. Although other craftsmen in Sheffield followed Huntman's lead, cast-steel could only be made in small quantities, so the use of steel was limited until the 1850s when further inventions led to the mass-production of cheap steel.

A view of Newcastle-upon-Tyne in the early nineteenth century.

The town of Hull, which may well deserve the third place among the English trading towns, has in the last few years risen to an almost unbelievable degree of prosperity through the extended trade and manufacture of Great Britain. In the town itself there are various works which deserve attention, among them are an oil mill, a porcelain factory, brick kilns and a **foundry**.

In the foundry, which consisted of some air-furnaces and a cupola furnace, the bellows of which were worked by a horse, all kinds of castings were made. In my presence a boiler with a capacity of a few hundred quarts was cast in sand. Shortly before casting, part of the iron accidentally escaped from the furnace; however, the shortage was immediately made up from another furnace, from which the workmen carried the iron in large ladles, and so filled the mould. They believed that this accident would have no effect on the boiler, and if this is so, it confirms still further the idea that in general English pig iron is taken to a much higher temperature than with us, and thus, perhaps more nearly approaches wrought iron in its nature.

At the shipyard I saw the cast-steel saws that I had admired in Sheffield, in general use. The largest were five feet long. Here, as at the new docks, work began at 7 o'clock in the morning, and finished at 6 o'clock in the evening. This is the usual working period in England and is adequate for anyone who wants to use his strength properly. In general, I observed that the English work not vigorously, but evenly.

In order to get from Hull on to the great post road to Newcastle-upon-Tyne, one must return to York. From York to Newcastle one travels through the towns of Easingwold, Thirsk and up to Durham. At Chester-le-Street, approximately halfway between Durham and Newcastle, one already begins to notice coal mines, which afterwards continue along the banks of the River Wear down into Sunderland. Near to Newcastle one comes to the famous deposits which are worked on both sides of the River Tyne. It is easy to understand how almost the whole of London is supplied with coal from this area and further substantial quantities are exported to the north, to France, to the Mediterranean and the West Indies. The best and most considerable seams of coal lie about 90 fathoms deep, almost horizontally and are rarely more than 5 feet thick. Above the town (to the west of Newcastle) the seams are less regular, and the coal in general worse, so that it sells for less than the coal mined in and below the town.

The inflow of water in all the mines around Newcastle is very considerable and is controlled by steam engines of 50, 60 and up to 100 horse-power. In order to hold back the water in the mine shaft, the walls are timbered or, which is now the most usual, lined with bricks or hewn sandstone. In some places the shafts are built of cast iron cylinders, of which one fits into the other, several fathoms deep. The cost of sinking and lining a shaft to the large coal seams which lie 90 fathoms or so deep, is reckoned at £6,000 to £8,000 sterling or more. Therefore they make shift to work underground without digging more vertical shafts for as long as they can, until there is no further ventilation and they must dig another vertical shaft. Such long passages underground demand a great number of horses. At Long Benton alone there are 85 horses.

WROUGHT IRON
Wrought iron means iron that has been worked on. This used to mean iron that had been heated and hammered in a forge. The heating and hammering made the iron much less brittle than cast iron and therefore it was stronger for making certain things such as spades and plough blades. Once iron could be puddled and rolled it was more generally called bar iron but essentially this had similar qualities to wrought iron. By 1800, 90 per cent of the demand for iron was for bar iron.

The transport of coal to the River Tyne is usually done on railways. Although these ways, if I am not mistaken, first came into use in the Newcastle district, they have not been brought to the perfection of those in Wales and some other places. On the other hand the mines here seem to be operated more systematically than elsewhere in the country. Among the various installations, there are in particular two of note, for bringing the coals from the mines down to the loading point on the River Tyne. One of them consists of an underground railway tunnel about three miles long through which the coals are brought out of the mine by horses and waggons. I was told this was, however, more costly than hauling coal to the surface by steam engines.

The other installation was an ingenious method of raising the coal from a deep mine by means of an iron rope half a mile long, drums, gearing and counterweights. The tubs of coal are pulled up the half mile slope and the empty tubs descend to the floor of the mine at the same time. There is a brake on the drum, by means of which the speed of ascent and descent can be moderated. They wanted to fit a **Watt governor** to this machine so that it did not need a man to work the brake, but it is not used any more, because the man who loads the waggons had nothing else to do during the up and down journeys except to work the brake.

Apart from the coalmines there are other industries which contribute to the prosperity of Newcastle-upon-Tyne. Among these are an ironworks producing high quality iron at Lemington, a **vitriol** works at Denton and a works distilling tar from coal near Denton, as well as other ironworks (some small ones making and repairing anchors and other

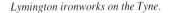

Lymington ironworks on the Tyne.

things for ships), foundries, powder mills, grinding mills and white lead works, spinning mills, potteries etc.

In a town where people are so occupied with extensive trading, mining and manufacture, there seems to be almost no time for the sciences. Yet a smaller version of the Royal Institution in London is being set up here. It has progressed so far that chemical and physical lectures are held on certain days of the week; also a fine library has been created, a collection of minerals purchased and several expensive instruments ordered. Within a few months enough money had been collected by subscription so that some public lectures could be started. Here, as in London, I found the lectures attended by people of all ranks, of every age, and by a large number of ladies, which latter likewise exhibited close attention, notwithstanding that some of them had quite innocently expected something different.

Before I left Newcastle I made an excursion to see the remarkable iron bridge over the River Wear at Sunderland. This is the largest and finest iron bridge which has yet been built anywhere. It is 236 feet long and so high that three masted vessels can sail under it with full sail. Everywhere in England one comes across engraved drawings, views and descriptions of the bridge, and at the inn where I stopped at midday, the bills were embellished with an engraved view of it.

On my departure from Newcastle I took the mailcoach to Berwick intending to stay there the night. When I arrived there, all the rooms were occupied on account of the forthcoming **Assizes**, and I therefore had to continue my journey through the night. Here I had the misfortune, for the first and last time on my journey through

England, to travel with a drunken driver, who, under the pretence of letting his horses recover their breath, increased his state of intoxication every time we stopped at an inn. The post escort (mail guard), who in this matter seemed to be a true comrade, was finally called into the coach to keep company where he manoeuvred so clumsily with his loaded gun and pistols that we were all certainly in greater danger from him than from being robbed by highway men. A passenger, according to the postal regulations, had the right to call for order, however, after I got possession of the gun, I considered it safer to let a small disorder pass than by my remonstrances perhaps give rise to a greater one.

CHAPTER 6

Scotland

EDINBURGH UNIVERSITY

Edinburgh University was founded in 1583. By the eighteenth century Scotland was famous for its education and people came to study there from all over Europe. Adam Smith was one of many famous men of the time who studied at Edinburgh and then became a professor at Glasgow University. Smith was a pioneer of the study of economics. He thought that a country was most likely to be successful if the workers specialized at what they did best. Thus it was more efficient for example, in a factory making pins, if one person cut the wire, the next sharpened it, the next put on the pin head and so on. This would be much quicker than one person making the whole pin himself. More pins would be made. More pins would be sold. Smith also believed that governments should interfere as little as possible in trading activities. This argument appealed to many of the businessmen and factory owners of the industrial revolution (including Josiah Wedgwood). They read Smith's book, *Wealth of Nations* with interest.

Edinburgh occupies a distinguished position among the towns of Great Britain not merely as the old capital of Scotland, but because it may vie with most European towns on account of its beautiful situation, its pleasing buildings and its extensive trade.

The University is too well known to need any description by me here. It is known that few universities in Europe have had more famous teachers in a shorter time. Foreigners who completed their studies here have never had cause to regret the time and expense and I attended a lecture in chemistry with the greatest pleasure. It was delivered with the tidiness which is usually observed in England and with such clarity that I, although I was less used to the language here, yet did not lose a single word.

I made excursions with two mineralogists into the mountains around Edinburgh. The rocks were interesting to a mineralogist but the mountains otherwise contain neither coal, metals nor other materials which were immediately connected with the purpose of my tour, with the exceptions of chalk and sandstone. Neither in the new nor in the old towns of Edinburgh are there, so far as I know, any important factories, except a large **distillery** and a place where the '**biscuit**' for genuine porcelain is painted and gilded. Since the spirit distillery is one of the largest and most developed chemical operations it must certainly attract the attention of an investigator of factories. Moreover the distilleries are among the few Scottish manufacturing establishments which can give an approximate idea of large-scale production. Other factories around the town are smaller and include various glassworks, foundries, salt boilers, soap and **soda** factories and paper mills.

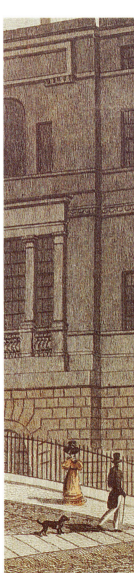

At Lasswade, I encountered a paper mill which interested me. The rollers which crushed the rags, and the washing machine, were driven by a steam engine, and the water was led into the works through iron pipes from a brook. The method was, so far as I could observe in the haste, different from that at Swedish paper mills. The rags were sorted, and cut on knives set upright for the purpose in tables fixed to the walls all round the room, which work was done by old people and children. After this the rags were taken to the washing machine, from which the coarser ones went immediately through all the rollers to the vat house, but the finer ones were put into the bleaching trough. This was in a special house on either side of a furnace in which six crucibles or earthenware pots, two and two together, could be comfortably set in and taken out. These pots, which were provided with heads from which porcelain pipes went into the trough, were filled with sulphuric acid, common salt and manganese dioxide in such proportions as to obtain a completely saturated hydrochloric acid [actually chlorine], which was evolved upon distillation, combined with the water in the paper pulp, and gave the

View of the south-east facade of Edinburgh University shortly after its completion in the 1820s.

latter desired whiteness in a short time. The prepared stuff was taken up as usual on moulds, on which a fine mesh of brass wire was stretched. Then it was laid between woollen cloths, pressed and then hung up to dry, scraped, treated with size, dried and pressed again. The scraping was done with special knives, sheet by sheet, in order to remove the small lumps and dust. This work was done mostly by young girls, who exhibited a skill therein, by which the English factory workers distinguish themselves from all others. The finished paper has a fine appearance and far surpasses the French and Swedish; it has, however, the same fault as even the best paper nowadays, in that it is more fragile and does not last as long as the old Dutch paper. Presumably this stems from nothing other than the now general use of rollers with knives, which cut through the threads of the rags, instead of the mills and stamps which were formerly used to break them up more along the length and breadth, whereby the old paper on drying became more cohesive and got a firmer web.

This is one of the many cases which prove that one often loses in the quality of goods what one gains in manufacturing price by speeding up the work. In such cases the manufacturer must weigh the pros and cons carefully, for if in the long run he can better dispose of a less good product at a lower price, I do not see why he should spend money upon its improvement, especially since the public is often more concerned with a good buy than a good product. This is quite a different matter from making and selling poor goods under a name with a good reputation.

During my stay around Edinburgh I also wanted to visit the famous ironworks at Carron, which lie near the mouth of the Forth and Clyde Canal. However, since one cannot under any circumstances get to see these works, I considered it advantageous to make a tour of Fifeshire in the company of Messrs Allan and Harden to whom I had been introduced in Edinburgh. Before we set off I did visit an ironworks belonging to Mr Caddell and Sons which used scrap iron, making it into sheets, spades, shovels and the like. A large amount of the scrap iron is bought in from Holland and consisted of old nails, horseshoes and a hundred and one other such things, which are there, as in France and England, partly picked up by poor people from the streets and rubbish dumps and partly collected from old ships and timber buildings.

After this visit we returned to Edinburgh and Mr Allan immediately suggested that he should bear me company on the return journey to Glasgow, through the western part of Scotland, Cumberland and as far as Liverpool. Although I knew from experience that one is sometimes hindered, even by the best of company, in looking at things as

COLLECTING SCRAP

Many people in Britain were very poor. Some of the very poorest earned a little money by collecting rubbish from the streets. All sorts of rubbish was collected and people specialized in different sorts. Some collected rags and some bones and some nails and horseshoes. Some even collected dogs' dirt in buckets from the streets to sell to the tanning yards for the processing of leather. Recycling is not new.

thoroughly as one would wish, I could not yet decline this offer which reduced the costs and opened the way for me to some good acquaintances.

On the same day as we left Edinburgh, we came to Wilsontown, an ironworks which belonged to Mr John Wilson of London. The first installations of this works which John Wilson began a few years ago in partnership with his brother William, are said to have cost £100,000. Finding that some of the refining methods were not profitable, John Wilson by 1802 had pulled down a part of the old works and installed puddling furnaces and rolling mills. A tourist cannot expect straight answers to improper questions, so I could not ask to be told the cost of this alteration, but from the knowledge I have, I would hazard a guess that, before it is all in working order, the costs may run to £30,000 or more. Although there are plentiful supplies of coal and ore here, and the transport of these materials can also be arranged more easily in time, it yet seems inconceivable how this works, which must take its iron more than two miles overland to the nearest port, can yield a return on the capital invested. However, Mr Wilson is a good patriot, and has sufficient steadfastness to

Dowlais rolling mills, drawing by C. W. Campion.

follow a plan which, without paying in the first years, gives an almost certain hope of high returns in the future, and through which, in any case, a place of refuge is prepared for many people who, otherwise than in wartime, would have to seek their living in foreign parts.

A few miles from Wilsontown, at [New] Lanark, we looked at a large cotton spinning mill which had been founded a few years before by a businessman in Glasgow, but which had now been sold to a London company. There were four buildings and for each a low overshot water wheel a few feet wide drove the whole of the machinery, which was made entirely of cast iron. In one of the large halls where the spinning was completed, 2,060 threads were spun at once. This mill is one of the largest in the kingdom, but there are many smaller ones around Glasgow, Liverpool and Manchester.

From here our route went via Hamilton, where we spent the night, and on to the Clyde ironworks, the largest iron foundry in Scotland, next to the Carron works. Near the works are a few coal mines, wherein ironstone likewise occurs and supplies are regarded as inexhaustible.

The town of Lanark, drawn by I. Clark and published in 1825.

The boring of cannon is done here, as everywhere in England, in the horizontal position. For drilling the **touch-hole**, Mr. Outram, the supervisor, had invented a small machine, concerning which he intended to apply for a patent. This machine could be moved quickly from one cannon to another by one workman and by its means the touch-hole could be given exactly any desired position and size in two or three minutes. In the foundry several ten- to twelve-year old boys were employed, who moulded small pans and other fine castings in sand with admirable skill. One of the lads pushed his daily wages higher than one of the older moulders was able to do.

We left Clyde and arrived in Glasgow. The short stay in this town did not allow me to see the many excellent works and factories which are situated here, among which are various large cotton spinning mills, muslin and calico factories, dyeworks etc. A recently founded factory, in which 150 workers were engaged daily in the finishing of genuine porcelain, with earthenware according to Wedgwood's invention, and other coarser kinds deserves attention, as does a muslin factory, which I accidentally managed to see, for the finishing of fine muslin. The purpose was to remove all the fluff which arises on the surface of the muslin in weaving. This purpose was served by a brick-built furnace four to five feet high, into which was fitted a cylinder of cast iron twelve to thirteen inches in diameter and a few feet long. By an ingenious means of rollers and cranks, the muslin could be wound on to the red hot cylinder thereby burning off the fluff. It is easy to see that a correctly gauged speed and an even movement is the main thing here, for if the fine muslin touches the iron cylinder only one or two seconds longer than it has to, it would certainly burst into flames. I later saw the same device used in Manchester with velveteen.

Glasgow has a very fine situation between the River Clyde and the Monkland Canal, which latter forms a branch of the Forth and Clyde Canal. Trade has greatly expanded here in the last few years, to which the new canal has certainly contributed, although people complain that voyages through it progress slowly, that the canal is too large for small barges and too small for ships etc. In the neighbourhood of Glasgow, especially at Paisley, are rich coalmines which are intensively worked.

We continued our journey from Hurlet to Kilmarnock and Sanquhar, and thence to the town of Dumfries, which is a fairly large town, mostly built of red sandstone. Immediately before the town on the way to Carlisle begin great plains, which extend 20 or 25 miles up to Gretna Green on the English border.

NEW LANARK

The cotton mill was founded in 1785 by David Dale with the support of Richard Arkwright, inventor of the spinning frame. The mills became famous when Robert Owen moved there. Owen was born in 1771 in Wales and went to school until the age of ten. He was then apprenticed to a clothier and did so well that he was appointed superintendant of a Manchester cotton mill at the age of nineteen. He made improvements and used new types of cotton. He soon became manager and a partner. Then he persuaded his partners to purchase the New Lanark mills.

In New Lanark there were 2,000 people, 500 of whom were children from poor houses, mostly orphans. Although they had been well treated, Owen wanted to do better. He set up welfare schemes, improved housing, restricted alcohol sales and started schools. People came to see the New Lanark mills from all over the world. When Svedenstierna visited in 1802 Owen was just starting.

The North West

The town of Carlisle, which lies near to the border, is one of the oldest in the country, more badly than well built, with long crooked alleys, but in a fine situation.

From Carlisle to the lead mines at Aldstone [Alston] Moor there are two ways. We were advised to take the longer route through the town of Penrith because of the difficulty of getting horses on the shorter one. On arrival in Penrith, no one would drive us without four horses to a post chaise. We had to spend at least three days at Aldstone Moor, and, because a post-chaise was not obtainable there, it looked as if we would have to keep the present one with us, and pay the expenses of the coachman and the horses. On a careful calculation the costs of this ran to £9, so we decided to go on foot and only to take with us a horse to carry the necessary articles and a man as a guide. Anyone whose health and strength do not permit of a journey on foot, and who has less time than we had, can make the journey in comfort with little cost, if he books a seat in one of the public coaches which go two or three times weekly between Carlisle and Newcastle, to Hexam [Hexham] from where there is a public road to Aldstone Moore, 35 miles at the most. I introduce this here, partly for the information of future tourists, partly as proof of the usefulness of being acquainted with the map, if one leaves the large highways of England.

Aldstone Moor is a small and badly built town, inhabited mainly by miners and other workers employed at the lead smelting works. The mines stretch for several miles and work was now proceeding on an exploratory gallery, which was said to stretch for several hundred fathoms into one of the most important minefields. This gallery, which already passes twice beneath the bed of the River Tyne, was so arranged that the water therein was always kept at a given level and thus ore and rubble could be transported on barges. The ore is taken to the smelting works, and here put, together with coal, into a hearth fifteen to eighteen inches deep. In smelting down in such a low hearth much lead evaporates, and it has been decided to install a smoke trap at one smelting works, less, however, to save lead than to lessen the fumes for the workmen, who seldom survive at this work for three or four years, and who all looked very sickly.

LEAD MINING

Lead is found in rock which has to be heated to extract the soft lead. It is used widely in roofing, making coffins, tanks, pipes etc. as it does not rust like iron, is easy to mould and shape and is most effective at keeping water out. It is in great demand in war time for bullets and ammunition of all kinds. Lead is poisonous and the poison accumulates in the body causing damage to the brain and nervous system.

From Aldstone Moor our way went back through Penrith, to the little town of Keswick, in the neighbourhood of which lies the famous graphite mine which belongs to the Hospital of Greenwich. So that the graphite does not fall to too low a price, the mine is only staffed and worked every seventh year, and was now closed down.

From here we made our way to Liverpool. Liverpool is now, in respect of extent and population, one of the most important towns in the world. Its commerce has in a space of fifteen to twenty years so noticeably increased that whereas Bristol, whose trade may be somewhat in decline, formerly had twice as much commerce as Liverpool, the proportions are now said to be reversed. This is attributed in part to the position, which is advantageous for overseas trade and for communication with the large inland manufacturing towns; and in part as a consequence of the industrious way of living and thrift of the inhabitants.

One needs only to be here for a short time to get an idea of the quantity of goods loaded and unloaded, of the numbers of arriving and departing ships, and of the value of the enormous stocks which are in the warehouse near the harbour. The war declared a few days before had, instead of retarding commerce, made it livelier, at least for a time. During the negotiations no safe speculation could be

Liverpool from Seacombe Boathouse, a watercolour by Michael Angelo Rooker c.1769.

The Bridgewater Canal is shown from left to right crossing the river Irwell by means of a viaduct (built by James Brindley in the mid-seventeenth century). Barges on the canal are pulled by horses on the towpath, while 'hobblers' pull a boat on the river below.

made; now, however, people had learnt by experience in the last war to take precautions, and this had taught that if one must, as a human being, sigh over the misfortune of war, the businessman can be very satisfied with the capital which war brings in. Among the ventures which engaged the inhabitants of Liverpool at this moment was the equipping of **privateering** vessels, which was done with such rapidity that five were already fit for sea before the declaration of war came here. In eight days afterwards fifteen others were fitting out, most of which returned from a short cruise with rich Dutch and French prizes. Also the **slave ships** present, of sixteen to eighteen guns, were said to have made a cruise before their departure to Africa.

A canal, which begins at Leeds in Yorkshire, runs through a stretch of some 80 miles in Lancashire and terminates near the harbour in a great basin where coal and other goods are unloaded. Various smaller canals are linked to this one and through the navigable rivers between Leeds and the Humber it opens to some extent a connection right across England. With other canals too the situation of the town is one of the most favourable for inland and foreign trade that can be imagined.

After a few days I travelled in the company of Mr Bourne from Liverpool to Manchester. This town has extended extraordinarily,

especially in the last fifteen years, through its cotton manufactures. Several circumstances have united to favour the growth of the cotton industry, among which the general use of the fine, white and light cotton fabric, which has almost supplanted silk throughout Europe, may deserve first place. Next to this comes the invention of the spinning machines. Almost all these machines are driven by steam engines. In order to carry away the coal smoke, which could take away from the cotton something of the dazzling whiteness given to it by artificial bleaching, the chimneys at most of the mills are taken up high above the roofs, and in some places arrangements are made to burn up the smoke during the heating. With such a large demand for coal, it is no small advantage that even at the present high prices, Manchester can have coal at about 50 per cent cheaper than the coal cost a little over 40 years ago, before the Duke of Bridgewater's Canal was finished, from whose coal mines practically the whole of Manchester is supplied.

Between Barton and Worsley the countryside is less level, and the canal is walled in or embanked in several places. At Worsley, a subterranean canal is taken to the coalmines. The coal is taken in waggons from the various working places in the mines and tipped into boats. Several of these boats, coupled together, are then taken to Worsley by men or horses through the underground canal, from where transport proceeds mostly to Manchester in larger boats. When the Duke of Bridgewater died a few years ago, his annual income from the canal, the coalmines, and some other properties, besides shares, was estimated at £120,000.

In consequence of the general suspicion in which all foreigners were held now that war had broken out, I decided to set off immediately for London. I took the so-called Opposition Coach to Derby and got only a glimpse of the countryside because I had allowed no more than six and a half hours to cover about fifty-four miles. At Derby I took a seat in the mail coach for London and after some weeks' stay in that city, I returned at the end of October on an English packet boat to the fatherland, when I immediately decided to publish a part of the notes I had made during my journey.

CANALS

Heavy goods are carried most easily by water. As iron and coal and manufactured goods became more important to Britain so water transport became more important in the eighteenth century. At first rivers were dredged and straightened but this was not enough. Canals soon followed. The first was the Sankey Brook in 1757 and the Duke of Bridgewater's Canal to carry coal from his mines to Manchester in 1761. These canals were so successful that in the 80 years to 1840 a whole network of canals were built all over the country. Until the coming of railways, canals carried the goods of the Industrial Revolution – coal, iron ore, cotton, wool, bricks, farm products and factory goods like Wedgwood's pottery.

Glossary

abutment buttress at end of bridge.

aqueduct bridge carrying water across a valley.

assizes sittings of a judge and jury on tour.

biscuit to do with porcelain – pottery that has been fired but not yet glazed.

blast furnace a smelting furnace into which hot air is blown.

bolt iron round bar iron.

castings anything cast in a mould.

consul the agent for a foreign country. For example, Brandström was a Swede living in Hull. He acted as Swedish consul and would help any Swedes visiting England. Sometimes there were consuls in each major city.

culvert an arched channel, usually made of bricks or stone to carry water under a road or railway.

cupola furnace furnace with domed top.

distillery a place where liquid is heated to form a vapour, then allowed to cool and condense in order to extract something. Distilleries particularly refer to the making of alcoholic spirits.

fathom an old measurement – originally the reach of a man's outstretched arms, later 6 feet (about 2 metres).

feldspar common mineral, found in granite and other rocks.

firing baking to a high temperature.

flanges raised edges.

flatiron an iron for smoothing creases from cloth.

foundry a place where metal is melted and cast in moulds.

glaze to cover with a thick, glassy covering.

guinea £1.05p

hoop iron thin, flat bar iron out of which hoops are made.

horsepower the power one horse can exert (this is taken as being 746 watts).

ingot a lump of unwrought or unworked metal, cast in a mould.

ironmaster man owning an ironworks.

ironstone iron ore or the rock in which iron is found.

kiln a large oven.

lathe a machine for turning and shaping wood and metal.

limekiln the furnace in which calcium carbonate is changed to lime.

lock dues payment for using the lock on a canal.

mortar a mixture of cement, sand and water.

patent an official document, granted by the government, giving a right or privilege. For example, Henry Cort was granted a patent for his puddling process; this meant that no one else could copy it for a certain number of years.

pig iron molten iron run into moulds called pigs.

plumbago graphite (mineral composed of carbon).

porcelain fine, semi-transparent earthenware.

post-chaise carriage drawn by horses, used as a long distance taxi by the rich.

powder mills where gunpowder was made.

privateering a private ship engaged to plunder enemy ships (pirates commissioned by the government of the day!)

Quaker a member of the Religious Society of Friends.

quarry an open pit where stone, slate, iron ore etc. is dug out.

refinery place where iron (or anything else) is made more pure.

seams to do with coal – bands of coal found between other rocks.

shareholder one who buys shares in a company, thereby sharing in the profits of the company.

slave ships ships that took guns, beads etc. to Africa where they were sold in exchange for slaves. The ships then sailed to the Americas and sold the slaves in return for tobacco, sugar etc.

smelting melting in order to separate metal from the ore it is found in.

soda sodium oxide used to make washing soda, baking soda etc.

stove a closed heating apparatus like an oven.

touch-hole the small hole of a cannon through which fire reaches the charge.

towpath path beside a canal for a horse to walk along when towing a barge.

translucent can see light shining through, not as clear as transparent.

ventilator chimney chimney to the surface to provide air deep in the mine. Usually there were two ventilator shafts. A fire was lit at the bottom of one shaft. This heated the air and caused it to rise up the shaft, thereby leaving an area of low pressure at the bottom of the shaft and in the mine. Cold, fresh air from the surface, rushed down the other ventilator shaft to equalize the air pressure. Thus fresh air was continually circulated through the mine.

vitriol sulphuric acid and related chemicals.

Watt governor a regulator for controlling speed, invented by James Watt.

wrought iron cast iron that has been heated and hammered.

Index

Numbers in *italic* type refer to captions; numbers in **bold** type refer to information boxes.